MW01155717

A gift given with love to:

....

....

....

From:

....

....

....

Fantastic! Thanks for letting me see this wonderful book. I'm looking
forward to encouraging parents to use this with their children!
Connie Dever, Wife of Mark Dever, Senior Pastor, Capitol Hill Baptist
Church, Washington D.C.

When God says it -He does it

Bible Prophecies Fulfilled by Jesus

Carine Mackenzie
Illustrated by Natascia Ugliano

CF4•K

Contents

1. Who Is Jesus?

The Israelites were God's special people. God spoke to them by the prophets. They warned them of sin, encouraged them to follow God and his commands, and told them of the promised Saviour – the Messiah.

The Scriptures of the Old Testament give many clues to the identity of the Messiah.

These Scriptures are helpful and encouraging to us too, giving us proof and confirmation that the Lord Jesus Christ is indeed God's Chosen One, God the Son who became man, born into this world to be the Saviour of his people.

People who knew the writings of Moses, the Psalms and the books of the Prophets would see in the life of Jesus the fulfilment of prophecies made hundreds of years before and recorded in God's Word.

Let's look at some of them.

2. The First Clue

Way back in the beginning of time, in the garden of Eden, God made a promise about the Saviour.

Adam and Eve had sinned by giving in to the temptation of the devil who came in the form of a serpent. God said to the serpent, 'I will put enmity between you and the woman, and between your offspring and her offspring; he shall bruise your head and you shall bruise his heel' (Genesis 3:15).

That was the first clue about the Saviour. He would be a man – not an angel. He would be born of a woman into this world. This man would completely destroy the devil in the end.

Throughout history, clues were given as to which family would be chosen as the family of the Saviour, sometimes called the Messiah or Anointed One, the expected King and Deliverer.

3. Blessing the Nations

God spoke to Abraham after he showed his faith in God. Abraham had been prepared to offer his son Isaac as a sacrifice to God. God spared him from doing this and blessed him greatly. God said, 'In your offspring (child) shall all the nations of the earth be blessed' (Genesis 22:18).

God was pointing to one particular child to be born many centuries later – Jesus Christ. You can read about this in Galatians 3:16 in your Bible.

God confirmed to Abraham that Isaac, his son, would be the one in the line of the promised Saviour. 'Through Isaac shall your offspring be named' (Genesis 21:12).

Which son of Isaac would be the ancestor of the Saviour? Jacob is mentioned, 'A star shall come out of Jacob, and a sceptre shall rise out of Israel' (Numbers 24:17).

4. The Family Tree

Jacob had many sons – which one would be chosen? When Jacob was near the end of his life, he gathered all his sons together and spoke to them. His remarks about Judah gave a hint about the promised Saviour. Look up Genesis 49:10 in your Bible.

Jeremiah, the prophet, foretold that the Saviour, would belong to the family of David. God said, 'I will raise up for David a righteous Branch, and he shall reign as king … he will be called: The LORD is our righteousness' (Jeremiah 23:5-6).

Jeremiah brought this message of hope to the nations of Israel and Judah and to us.

This promise was fulfilled in the Lord Jesus Christ whose name means Saviour, 'for he will save his people from their sins' (Matthew 1:21).

All through history, God was taking care of the family line of the Messiah. Careful note was made of Jesus' family. If you have ever tried to trace your family tree, you do well if you can go back three or four generations. In the first chapter of Matthew we can read a list of Jesus' ancestors – highlighting Abraham and David. Luke traces Jesus' family from Joseph his legal father, right back to Adam.

5. Jesus' Mother

Very specific details were prophesied in the Old Testament about the birth of the Saviour, so that when he did come, people could be confident that he was indeed the one sent by God. The most unusual one came from the prophet Isaiah, 'Therefore the Lord himself will give you a sign.

Behold, the virgin shall conceive and bear a son, and shall call his name Immanuel' (Isaiah 7:14).

This amazing statement was proved to be true when Mary was found to be expecting a child when she was still a virgin.

6. A Little Place

Micah prophesied that the Messiah would be born in Bethlehem. 'But you, O Bethlehem Ephrathah, who are too little to be among the clans of Judah, from you shall come forth for me one who is to be ruler in Israel …' (Micah 5:2).

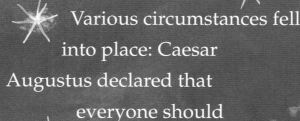

Various circumstances fell into place: Caesar Augustus declared that everyone should be taxed.

Joseph came from the family of David so he had to go to Bethlehem to pay his taxes.

Joseph and Mary made the journey from Nazareth to Bethlehem and there Jesus was born.

Hosea prophesied, 'out of Egypt I called my son' (Hosea 11:1).

How could the promised Saviour come from Bethlehem and Egypt? The young child Jesus was in danger. Herod the ruler was jealous at the thought of the king of the Jews being born. God warned Joseph in a dream to take Jesus and his mother to safety in Egypt. They stayed there until Herod died and it was safe to return to Israel. Then they settled in Nazareth – an obscure, despised place. A Nazarene was a despised person. Isaiah mentions that the Messiah would be despised and rejected by people.

God's amazing providence was overruling every detail.

7. Poor and Despised

Did the life of Jesus match up to the description of the coming Messiah in the Old Testament? The prophet Isaiah gave many clues about the coming Saviour.

He would be poor and insignificant, like a root sticking out of dry ground, not beautiful. Men would despise him and not think him at all important. Read about this in Isaiah 53:2-3.

Jesus was poor: he did not have a house of his own. 'Foxes have holes,' he said, 'and birds of the air have nests, but the Son of Man (i.e. Jesus) has nowhere to lay his head' (Luke 9:58).

Some people were offended when they heard his amazing teaching. 'Who does he think he is? He is just a carpenter's son. We know his brothers.' He was despised and given no place.

There was no pomp or show in Jesus' life. He was modest and meek in all he did and said, according to Matthew 12:18-21. Isaiah also foretold that in his prophecy. 'He will not cry aloud or lift up his voice, or make it heard in the street' (Isaiah 42:2).

8. Tender and True

What was Jesus like? He was tender and compassionate and kind in many ways – dealing with sinners, children, sick people, ignorant people. He compared himself to a good shepherd leading and caring for his flock. Isaiah foretold that the Messiah would tend his flock like a shepherd, and gather the lambs in his arms, carry them close to his heart and lead those with young. You can read this in Isaiah 40:11.

The man Jesus fitted this picture exactly.

Jesus is the truth. No lies or deceit ever came from his mouth. All he said was absolutely true and fair. Even that detail was foretold by Isaiah, 'there was no deceit in his mouth' (Isaiah 53:9).

9. Preaching and Parables

Parables are stories with a spiritual meaning. Much of Jesus' teaching was by parables – stories like the Good Samaritan and the Sower. He did this in order to fulfil the prophecy from Psalm 78. You can read about this in your Bible in Matthew 13:34-35.

Isaiah foretold that the Messiah would make the blind see, the deaf hear, the lame walk and the dumb sing for joy (Isaiah 35:5-6). Jesus did amazing miracles of healing.

Jesus gave Bartimaeus his sight back. He healed a man who was deaf and dumb. Read about these miracles in Mark 10:46–52 and Mark 7:31-37. Many were healed and knew that Jesus performed miracles. Even the chief priests and the Pharisees admitted, 'What are we to do? For this man performs many signs' (John 11:47).

Jesus preached in the synagogue in Nazareth, first reading from the book of Isaiah, from what we call chapter 61 verses 1-2.

'The Spirit of the Lord is upon me because he has anointed me to proclaim good news to the poor.

He has sent me to proclaim liberty to the captives and recovery of sight to the blind, to set at liberty those who are oppressed, to proclaim the year of the Lord's favour' (Luke 4:16-19).

After he finished reading, Jesus plainly said, 'Today this Scripture has been fulfilled in your hearing' (Luke 4:21). Jesus was claiming to be the Messiah spoken of in the book of Isaiah. As he preached, the people were amazed at his gracious words. But by the end of his sermon all the congregation were angry and drove him out of town.

10. Victory at Last!

There was a lot of opposition to Jesus. Even his own brothers did not believe in him, as you can see in John 7:5. In the first chapter of John we read that Jesus came to his own people and they did not receive him. David spoke about the coming Messiah in the Psalms and said that he would be a 'stranger' to his brothers and an 'alien' to his mother's sons (Psalm 69:8).

Isaiah prophesied that he would be despised and rejected by men. Jesus would have known the Scriptures very well and would have realised they were speaking about him.

Jesus warns us that the world will hate those who follow and trust him. 'If the world hates you, know that it has hated me before it hated you' (John 15:18-25).

The Lord Jesus is the one who is most worthy of love and reverence, but wicked men hated him without good cause. Jesus knew that was the case because it had been prophesied in the Psalm of David. 'More in number than the hairs of my head are those who hate me without cause' (Psalm 69:4).

The Jewish rulers rejected Jesus. They did not believe that he was the Messiah, the Son of God, come to do God's work of salvation.

The psalmist had spoken long before in a poetic way of the treatment by the authorities of God's Son. 'The stone that the builders rejected has become the cornerstone' (Psalm 118:22). Jesus referred to this verse in his teaching. Even although he would be rejected by the Jewish authorities, he would at last have the victory and be the important cornerstone of the church of God.

11. Suffering and Betrayal

Many prophecies from the Old Testament were fulfilled in just twenty-four hours at the time of Jesus' death.

In the Garden of Gethsemane he suffered intensely. His agony of soul was so great as he faced God's wrath for sin, that his sweat was like great drops of blood. David describes the experience of the Messiah when he writes about being 'poured out like water' and the heart melting 'like wax' (Psalm 22:14).

Jesus' suffering was not for himself but for the sin of others, his own people. He came to the world to serve and to give his life as a 'ransom for many' (Matthew 20:28).

Isaiah spoke for God's people when he said, 'He was pierced for our transgressions; he was crushed for our iniquities' (Isaiah 53:5).

The good news of the gospel is that 'Christ died for the ungodly' (Romans 5:6).

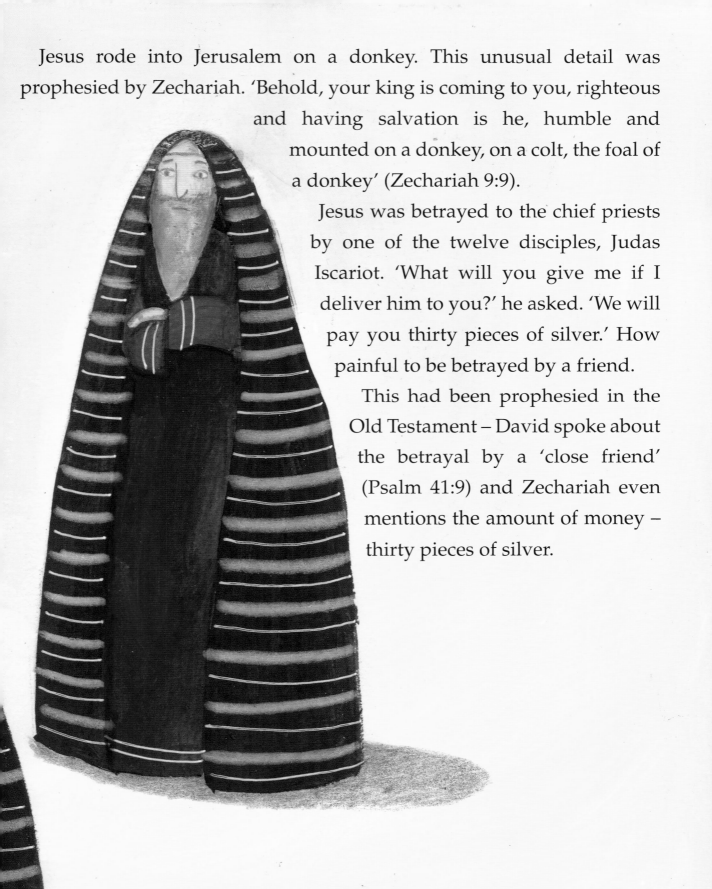

Jesus rode into Jerusalem on a donkey. This unusual detail was prophesied by Zechariah. 'Behold, your king is coming to you, righteous and having salvation is he, humble and mounted on a donkey, on a colt, the foal of a donkey' (Zechariah 9:9).

Jesus was betrayed to the chief priests by one of the twelve disciples, Judas Iscariot. 'What will you give me if I deliver him to you?' he asked. 'We will pay you thirty pieces of silver.' How painful to be betrayed by a friend.

This had been prophesied in the Old Testament – David spoke about the betrayal by a 'close friend' (Psalm 41:9) and Zechariah even mentions the amount of money – thirty pieces of silver.

12. Strike the Shepherd

There was another painful experience for the Lord Jesus. He was deserted by his disciples – they all forsook him and fled. The prophet Zechariah spoke about that too: 'Strike the shepherd and the sheep will be scattered' (Zechariah 13:7).

False witnesses came forward and told lies about Jesus, to get him into trouble with the authorities. David had foretold this in Psalm 109: 'Wicked and deceitful mouths are opened against me, speaking against me with lying tongues.'

When faced with these lies, Jesus remained silent. You can read this story for yourself in Matthew 26:57-68. Just as Isaiah had said long before: 'He was oppressed, and he was afflicted, yet he opened not his mouth' (Isaiah 53:7).

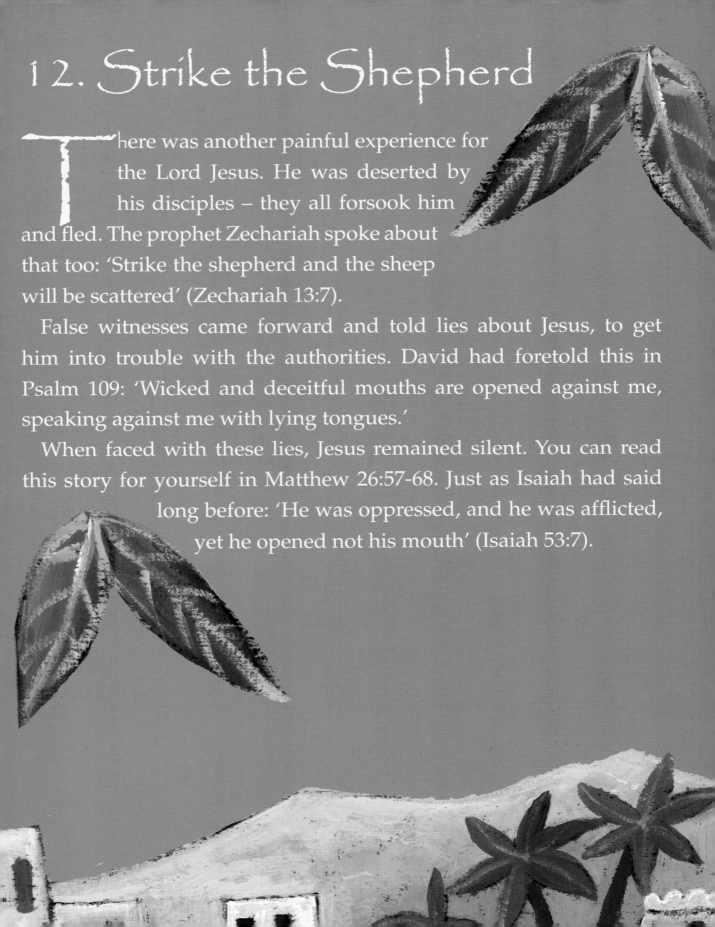

13. Father Forgive Them

The people standing by, watching the crucifixion of Jesus, probably thought he was a common criminal who deserved his punishment. But they were actually witnessing the most momentous event of history – God the Son who had become a man, taking the punishment for the sin of his people. Many details of that event had been prophesied hundreds of years before.

Psalm 22 told that his hands and feet would be pierced, that he would be forsaken by God the Father and that he would be mocked.

Jesus called out 'I thirst' on the cross so that the prophecy of Psalm 69 would be fulfilled. They gave him vinegar to drink which had been foretold by David in the Psalms too. Read Psalm 69:21.

In the midst of his suffering Jesus prayed for the soldiers who were nailing him to the cross. 'Father, forgive them, for they know not what they do' (Luke 23:34). Isaiah told that the Messiah would 'make intercession' (or pray for) the transgressors (Isaiah 53:12).

Jesus died beside two thieves who were also crucified. Isaiah had said, 'He would be numbered with the transgressors' (Isaiah 53:12).

14. Darkness in Daylight

After the soldiers had nailed Jesus to the cross, they took his garment, divided it into four pieces and each took a bit. His tunic was made of one piece of material so instead of tearing it, they cast lots to see who would get it. That incident was foretold exactly in Psalm 22:18.

When Jesus was on the cross, darkness covered the land from 12 noon until 3 o'clock in the afternoon – an unusual and frightening occurrence. Amos in his prophecy told that that would happen. 'On that day,' declares the Lord God, 'I will make the sun go down at noon and darken the earth in broad daylight.' (Amos 8:9).

When the soldiers came to break the legs of the three men being crucified, to hasten their deaths, they found that Jesus was dead already. So they did not break his legs. This fulfilled the Scripture from Psalm 34:20, 'He keeps all his bones, not one of them is broken.'

15. Begging for a Body

Two men went to Pilate to beg for the body of Jesus. One was Nicodemus and the other Joseph of Arimathea. Jesus' body was taken down from the cross. Joseph of Arimathea was a rich man. He placed the body in his own new tomb, cut out of the rock. No other body had ever been buried in this tomb before.

This fulfilled Isaiah's prophecy: 'They made his grave . . . with a rich man in his death' (Isaiah 53:9).

16. He is Risen!

How amazing it is that Jesus triumphed over death and the grave and rose again to life. 'He is not here. He is risen,' the angels told the women who came to the tomb. The risen Lord Jesus appeared to his disciples, Mary Magdalene and other women, two walking to Emmaus and even 500 people on one occasion.

One Psalm mentions Jesus' resurrection. 'You will not abandon me to the grave, or let your holy one see decay' (Psalm 16:10).

Jesus' resurrection proves that he is God. Our bodies too will be raised back to life. The resurrection of Jesus shows us that he has defeated death and hell.

17. The Ascension

The risen Lord Jesus and his disciples went to the Mount of Olives near Bethany. He raised his hands over them and blessed them and then as the disciples looked on, Jesus ascended into heaven.

David, in Psalm 68, spoke about this momentous event. 'You ascended on high, leading a host of captives in your train and receiving gifts among men . . .' (Psalm 68:18).

Jesus Christ returned to his Father and was glorified – the final proof that his work was completed. The verse in Psalm 68 refers to the victory of Christ as King and Conqueror, receiving the gifts promised to him for his church – like pastors, evangelists, teachers.

18. Prophet, Priest and King!

What is Jesus doing now? He is now seated at the right hand of God the Father, a place of unique honour, with authority over angels and powers in heaven and earth. Our prophet, the ascended Christ, is teaching us by his Word today.

'The LORD says to my Lord, "Sit at my right hand until I make your enemies your footstool."' Read about this in Psalm 110. David was not speaking about himself, but about Christ ascended in heaven.

Jesus is our Priest in heaven. He does not make any sacrifice as he did that already on the cross, but he is continually praying for his people. 'He shall be a priest on his throne,' said Zechariah, the prophet, about Jesus Christ.

Jesus is our king in heaven. The angel told Mary before he was born that he would be the 'Son of the Most High'. The Lord would give him the throne and there would be no end to his kingdom (Luke 1:32-33).

Isaiah prophesied this wonderful truth too. 'The government shall be upon his shoulder . . . of the increase of his government and of peace there will be no end, on the throne of David and over his kingdom' (Isaiah 9:6-7).

19. Jesus' Second Coming

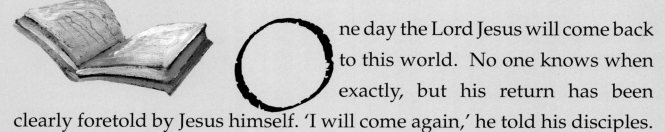

One day the Lord Jesus will come back to this world. No one knows when exactly, but his return has been clearly foretold by Jesus himself. 'I will come again,' he told his disciples.

The Old Testament also prophesied that the Son of Man (the Lord Jesus) would come to earth not as a helpless baby, but as a conquering king with dominion over all peoples (Daniel 7:13-14).

Zechariah prophesied that, 'On that unique day the LORD my God will come, and all the holy ones with him' (Zechariah 14:5).

That prophecy is yet to be fulfilled, but it will be, as surely as all the others.

'Surely I am coming soon,' John heard Jesus say in his Revelation. 'Come, Lord Jesus,' was John's response.

20. Yesterday, Today ... and Forever

God never changes. Jesus Christ is the same yesterday, today and forever. God's Word is true and sure and with no errors. All that God said through the prophets and the psalmist about his Son the Messiah, has come to pass in the life of the Lord Jesus and is being fulfilled in what Christ is doing now. This is the God we should worship and the Saviour we should trust.

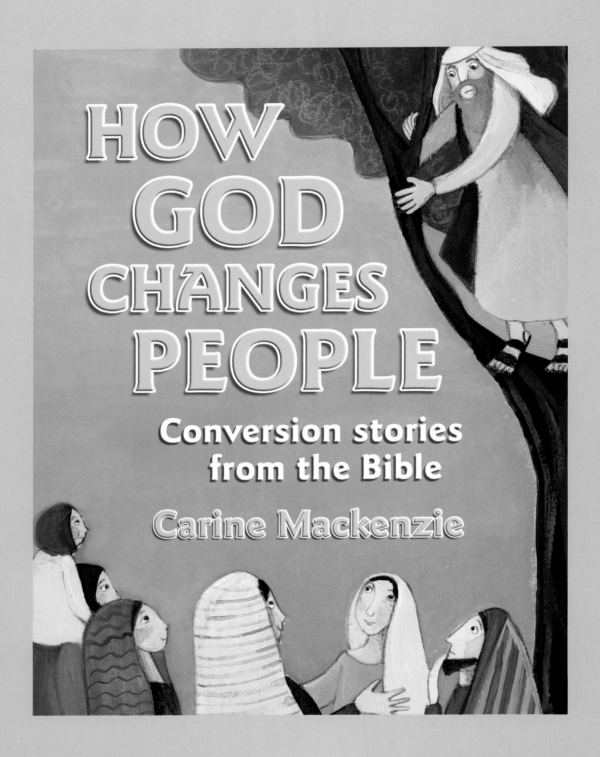

HOW GOD CHANGES PEOPLE
by Carine Mackenzie

A sneaky little thief meets Jesus and then he starts giving away his money instead – that's Zacchaeus. A ruthless thug chases down Christians, but after a run in with the risen Lord, he joins forces with the people he once hated – that's Paul. A young woman sits on the river bank, when she hears the Word of God, a quiet change warms her heart and another sinner is saved, a life changed and an eternity secured – that's Lydia. These people and others in this book were all changed by God through his Word. And we can read about them in his Word – the Bible.

ISBN: 978-1-84550-822-7

REVIEWS

Love! Love! Love this book! Carine helps children see how God works salvation in many different kinds of people and that he can work salvation in them, too!

Connie Dever Wife of Mark Dever, Senior Pastor,
Capitol Hill Baptist Church, Washington D.C.

None of us are born Christians – we must be born again. Carine shows the need for repentance and faith in Jesus in each biblical story she recounts. *How God Changes People* will most certainly encourage children to think about what it means to be saved. The illustrations will delight their eyes, and the stories will delight their souls.

Keri Folmar Wife of John Folmar,
Pastor of the United Christian Church of Dubai

Carine retells what happened and happens when people meet the Lord. Engagingly written, and beautifully illustrated, *How God Changes People* is a book every family will enjoy.

Sinclair B. Ferguson, Senior Minister
First Presbyterian Church of Columbia

From the first picture, where even the robin looks startled at the sound of breaking glass, this is a lovely book for all ages. It cleverly brings together New Testament people who were changed by meeting Jesus. It quietly challenges the reader: 'Has He changed me yet?' It puts a hunger in their hearts to become part of Jesus' family.

Helen Roseveare, Author and Speaker

This book is a great reminder of people in the Bible who were completely changed by an encounter with Jesus. Beautifully illustrated, faithful to the Bible, and (refreshingly for a children's book) the stories are well applied.

Stuart Chaplin, Keswick 4 Kids Team Leader

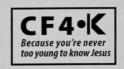

Christian Focus Publications publishes books for adults and children under its four main imprints: Christian Focus, CF4K, Mentor and Christian Heritage. Our books reflect our conviction that God's Word is reliable and Jesus is the way to know him, and live for ever with him.

Our children's publication list includes a Sunday School curriculum that covers pre-school to early teens, and puzzle and activity books. We also publish personal and family devotional titles, biographies and inspirational stories that children will love.

If you are looking for quality Bible teaching for children then we have an excellent range of Bible stories and age-specific theological books. From pre-school board books to teenage apologetics, we have it covered!

Find us at our web page: www.christianfocus.com

10 9 8 7 6 5 4 3 2 1

© Copyright 2014 Carine Mackenzie

ISBN: 978-1-78191-322-2

Published by Christian Focus Publications,
Geanies House, Fearn, Tain, Ross-shire,
IV20 1TW, Scotland, U.K.

Cover design: Daniel van Straaten

Illustrations by Natascia Ugliano

Printed in China